100 SEO Tips

Copyright by M R Fell

All rights reserved. Reproduction and distribution are forbidden. No part of this publication shall be reproduced, stored in a retrieval system, or transmitted by any other means, electronic, mechanical, photocopying, recording, or otherwise, without written permission from the publisher.

This publication is designed to provide accurate and authoritative information with regard to the subject matter covered. It is sold with the understanding that the author and the publisher are not engaged in rendering legal, intellectual property, accounting or other professional advice. If legal advice or other professional assistance is required, the services of a competent professional should be sought.

The author and and distributor individually or corporately, do not accept any responsibility for any liabilities resulting from the actions of any parties involved.

Introduction

This ebook will give you 100 search engine techniques. The competition is fierce in the search engines. In order to get your web site or blog ranked high you need all the SEO techniques you can handle from this list. But the great thing is the search engine is also one big search engine optimization school. You can study millions of high rank web sites and model their techniques to use on your web site.

1) You might add keywords/phrases in the html title tag. You could also model other high ranked blog site's SEO tactics.

2) You can have good linking structure. You might also clone other top listed video site's search engine tips.

3) You should insert keywords/phrases in the html body copy. You can also imitate other leading world news site's optimization methods.

4) You could purchase quality web hosting. You may also fabricate other number one wiki site's SEO concepts.

5) You may use a fast loading web site. You should also mirror other top 10 web site template site's search engine ideas.

6) You might place keywords/phrases in bold typeface. You could also copy other hierarchy portal site's optimization advice.

7) You can affix keywords/phrases in header tags. You might also pattern other high traffic web directory site's SEO instructions.

8) You should use quality web site links. You can also duplicate other top of the list web based software site's search engine loopholes.

9) You could submit link viral freebies to other sites. You may also reproduce other #1 yellow page site's optimization outlines.

10) You may add keyword/phrase image names. You should also simulate other top position web based book site's SEO checklists.

11) You might use quality internal linking. You could also study other uppermost ranked virtual world site's search engine models.

12) You can insert keyword/phrases image alts. You might also mold other first placed video sharing site's optimization plans.

13) You should refreshed your content regularly. You can also portray other upper listed video sales letter site's SEO steps.

14) You could get authority back links. You may also match other highest listed web ring site's search engine recipes.

15) You may use doorway pages. You should also generate other prime position top list directory site's optimization schemes.

16) You might place keywords/phrases in the domain name. You could also create other top five squeeze page site's SEO resources.

17) You can use SEO optimization software. You might also similar other popular placed sports site's search engine analysis.

18) You should add keywords/phrases in the web page name. You can also use other high ranked software directory site's optimization recommendations.

19) You could write keyword/phrases in the page folder. You may also attain other top listed social networking site's SEO links.

20) You may insert keyword/phrases in link names. You should also form other leading social media site's search engine solutions.

21) You might submit linked audio to other sites. You could also make other number one service site's optimization directions.

22) You can join back link exchanges. You might also produce other top 11 self improvement site's SEO maps.

23) You should get keyword/phrase name back links. You can also learn other hierarchy search engine site's search engine procedure.

24) You could use good ratio keyword/phrases in your content. You may also review other high traffic self help site's optimization descriptions.

25) You may type keywords/phrases in the Meta description tag. You should also add other top of the list sales letter site's SEO profile.

26) You might get quality back links. You could also incorporate other #2 resources site's search engine fixes.

27) You can use a good sized web page. You might also model other top position report site's optimization hints.

28) You should get tons of black links. You can also clone other uppermost ranked real estate listings site's SEO help.

29) You could make a lot related linked pages. You may also imitate other first placed question/answer site's search engine shortcuts.

30) You may allow visitor to add comments. You should also fabricate other upper listed proxy's site's optimization clues.

31) You might use original content. You could also mirror other highest listed profile site's SEO strategies.

32) You can purchase quality back links. You might also copy other prime position product review site's search engine commentary.

33) You should hire a SEO expert or service. You can also pattern other top five product catalog site's optimization formulas.

34) You could use quality site maps. You may also duplicate other popular placed web hosting site's SEO coaching.

35) You may submit linked videos to other sites. You should also reproduce other high ranked product site's search engine consulting.

36) You might use keyword/phrase named videos. You could also simulate other top listed picture sharing site's optimization explanations.

37) You can use balanced placement of back links. You might also study other leading personal site's SEO shortcuts.

38) You should link to good root domains. You can also mold other number one payment processor site's search engine keywords.

39) You could use gateway pages. You may also portray other top 12 organizational site's optimization processes.

40) You may create and link to many related mini sites. You should also match other hierarchy opt-in giveaway site's SEO blueprints.

41) You might use rewritten related PLR content. You could also generate other high traffic online service site's search engine templates.

42) You can allow visitors to add content. You might also create other top of the list online mall site's optimization systems.

43) You should start an affiliate program for links. You can also similar other #3 online game site's SEO suggestions.

44) You could create a content directory. You may also use other top position online auction site's search engine rules.

45) You may purchase high traffic expired domain names. You should also attain other uppermost ranked offline store site's optimization tricks.

46) You might use related news content or feeds. You could also form other first placed music sharing site's SEO techniques.

47) You can submit linked articles to other sites. You might also make other upper listed movie listings site's search engine factors.

48) You should research the keywords/phrases. You can also produce other highest listed mobile device site's optimization tutorials.

49) You could trade links with other targeted web sites. You may also learn other prime position mini site's SEO solutions.

50) You may partner with a top web site owner. You should also review other top five micro blog site's search engine information.

51) You might avoid over penalties for optimization. You could also add other popular placed membership site's optimization tactics.

52) You can use targeted keywords. You might also incorporate other high ranked map/directions site's SEO tips.

53) You should submit your site to all the search engines. You can also model other top listed local news site's search engine methods.

54) You could link to good page ranked sites. You may also clone other leading links page site's optimization concepts.

55) You may avoid using too many links on your page. You should also imitate other number one joint venture site's SEO ideas.

56) You might share linked pictures on sharing sites. You could also fabricate other top 13 instant commission site's search engine advice.

57) You can submit linked product reviews to to other sites. You might also mirror other hierarchy humor site's optimization instructions.

58) You should submit your site to all the web directories. You can also copy other high traffic how to site's SEO loopholes.

59) You could join linked banner exchanges. You may also pattern other top of the list graphic directory site's search engine outlines.

60) You may post link answers/questions on those sites. You should also duplicate other #4 government site's optimization checklists.

61) You might use bold or italicize keywords. You could also reproduce other top position gossip site's SEO models.

62) You can create linked auctions on auction sites. You might also simulate other uppermost ranked freelancer directory site's search engine plans.

63) You should use relevant content with keyword/phrases. You can also study other first placed freebie directory site's optimization steps.

64) You could design your site for specific search engines. You may also mold other upper listed free email site's SEO recipes.

65) You may submit linked press releases to sites. You should also portray other highest listed forum site's search engine schemes.

66) You might link and get back links to highly branded sites. You could also match other prime position fire sale site's optimization resources.

67) You can use different but related words. You might also generate other top five file sharing site's SEO analysis.

68) You should placed link pay per click advertising. You can also create other popular placed fan page site's search engine recommendations.

69) You could create and link to foreign language versions of your site. You may also similar other high ranked event listing site's optimization links.

70) You may submit multiple domain names for the same site. You should also use other top listed educational site's SEO solutions.

71) You might submit link post top forums. You could also attain other leading ecommerce site's search engine directions.

72) You can beware of your keyword density. You might also form other number one eBook directory site's optimization maps.

73) You should buy search engine optimization courses. You can also make other top 14 donation site's SEO procedures.

74) You could avoid web site crashes during sales. You may also produce other hierarchy dime sale site's search engine descriptions.

75) You may avoid using to much flash or java script. You should also learn other high traffic dictionary site's optimization profile.

76) You might use relevant keyword/phrase with inbound/outbound links. You could also review other top of the list diary site's SEO fixes.

77) You can submit link resumes on sites. You might also add other #5 dating site's search engine hints.

78) You should avoid being intimated be high rank sites. You can also incorporate other top position contextual ad content site's optimization help.

79) You could use misspell keywords/phrases. You may also model other uppermost ranked contest directory site's SEO shortcuts.

80) You may fix broken links on your web site. You should also clone other first placed content rating site's search engine clues.

81) You might create a mobile phone version of your site. You could also imitate other upper listed content archive site's optimization strategies.

82) You can place link classified ads on web sites. You might also fabricate other highest listed computer file storing site's SEO commentary.

83) You should submit linked post to social networks. You can also mirror other prime position company branding site's search engine formulas.

84) You could use shorten urls with relevant keyword/phrases. You may also copy other top five community site's optimization coaching.

85) You may interview high ranked web site owners. You should also pattern other popular placed classified ad site's SEO consulting.

86) You might avoid giving up to get a higher rank. You could also duplicate other high ranked chat room site's search engine explanations.

87) You can be aware of the word count of your pages. You might also reproduce other top listed celebrity site's optimization shortcuts.

88) You should offer to mange a site for a top web site owner. You can also simulate other leading career/job directory site's SEO keywords.

89) You could avoid using republished content. You may also study other number one bookmarking site's search engine processes.

90) You may use multiple domain types for the same site. You should also mold other top 15 blog plug in directory site's optimization blueprints.

91) You might track your SEO results and analytics. You could also portray other hierarchy blog hosting site's SEO templates.

92) You can give business linked testimonials. You might also match other high traffic auto responder site's search engine systems.

93) You should use services/account to the search engines you submit too. You can also generate other top of the list automobile for sale listings site's optimization suggestions.

94) You could submit link blog post to other sites. You may also create other #6 audio sharing site's SEO rules.

95) You may use keyword/phrases sub headings. You should also similar other top position audio sale letter site's search engine tricks.

96) You might use SEO web site scripts. You could also use other uppermost ranked article directory site's optimization techniques.

97) You can create and link to related blogs. You might also attain other first placed app directory site's SEO factors.

98) You should use keywords in your ad copy. You can also form other upper listed affiliate program site's search engine tutorials.

99) You could keep track of your competitions ranks. You may also make other highest listed adult site's optimization solutions.

100) You may use outsourced services for SEO. You should also produce other prime position about me site's SEO information.

Some Recommended Marketing Tools For You to Use

7 Zip: http://7-zip.org - an open source, free alternative to WinZip.

Winrar: http://www.rarlab.com/download.htm - Free Compression Tool for all types, compatible with a lot formats.

Skype: http://skype.com
Make free calls over the internet to other people on Skype. Chat and make Conference Calls for Free.

VLC Media Player: http://videolan.org/vlc - Media player capable of reading most audio and video formats.

Windows Movie Maker Live:
http://go.microsoft.com/fwlink/?LinkID=255475 – The most common windows movie maker tool you can get. User friendly interface with lots of basic features.

Adobe Reader: http://get.adobe.com/reader Used to view and print PDF files.

Nitro-PDF Reader: http://www.nitroreader.com/download/

PDF to Word Converter: http://pdftoword.com
Easily create editable Word Doc files from PDF content – for legit purposes only! :-)

Evernote: http://evernote.com
Scan your notes, receipts, etc ... it will OCR the content, save it, and make it searchable for sharing)

Chrome: https://www.google.com/intl/fil/chrome/browser/ - Mostly used browser, lots of features and sync all web data to its broad set of functions.

Firefox: http://mozilla.com/firefox - Alternate web browser.

Internet Marketing Blog: http://kevinfahey.net - Internet marketing blog sharing tips and tricks on list building, plr and affiliate marketing.

BrowserShots: http://browsershots.org Use this site to view how your website look in various browsers.

CamStudio: http://camstudio.org
Lets you record all screen & audio activity on your computer and create video files.

Down For Everyone Or Just Me :
http://downforeveryoneorjustme.com Is your site down? Use this tool to see if your website is down for other people.

FileZilla: http://filezilla-project.org Open source FTP program for uploading files to your host.

Kompozer: http://kompozer.net A free to HTML editor.

GIMP: http://gimp.org
An open source program used to create & edit - free alternative to Photoshop.

Open Office: http://openoffice.org Free document editing software.

Pixie: http://nattyware.com/pixie.php
Great for web designers - just point to a color and it will tell you the code value for that color.

Roboform: http://roboform.com Easily & safely manage your passwords.

ShortKeys: http://shortkeys.com
Allows you to set up replacement text or paragraphs for any user defined keystrokes.

TimeLeft: http://nestersoft.com/timeleft
A countdown, reminder, clock, alarm clock, stopwatch, timer, & web countdown tool.

My Little Piggy App: http://mylittlepiggyapp.com – A free mobile banking app to help your kids save money through doing chores, thus rewarding them with the benefits.

Web Social Mania Mobile Apps:
http://websocialmania.com/apps/ - Get Access to Free Readable PLR Products direct to your smartphone and More. You won't need any PDF reader to install.

High Mobi: http://high-5.mobi – Free Sms use, send messages to Facebook, twitter, high-five etc. for free.

Best Private Label Rights Membership : http://downloadplrproducts.com Over 1500 Private Label Rights Products with quick advanced search features and large database updated weekly.

Elite Group 2012: http://elitegroup2012.com – A Social Group Dedicated to help fellow internet marketers a kick start to their income.

Social Media N SEO Services: http://socialmedianseo.com/services/ – A Social Service dedicated to help boost your social marketing needs.

Web Social Mania: http://websocialmania.com – Facebook likes, twitter followers and YouTube Views.

Your SEO Services: http://yourseoservices.net – Done For You Seo Services

WordPress Conversion Tracker: http://wp-conversiontracker.com – Wordpress plugin that helps you track your links, easily organize and manage link tracking.

www.ingramcontent.com/pod-product-compliance
Lightning Source LLC
Chambersburg PA
CBHW081823170526
45167CB00008B/3514